# 6 THINGS
# I LEARNED THE
# HARD
# WAY

**GARY KEESEE**

**6 Things I Learned the Hard Way**

Unless otherwise noted, all Scriptures are from the New International Version® (NIV)® of the Holy Bible. Copyright © 1973, 1978, 1984 by Biblica, Inc.™ All rights reserved worldwide.

Scripture quotations marked (AMP) are from the Amplified® Bible, Copyright © 1954, 1958, 1962, 1964, 1965, 1987 by The Lockman Foundation. Used by permission.

ISBN: 978-1-945930-08-9

Published by Free Indeed Publishers.
Distributed by Faith Life Now.

Faith Life Now
P.O. Box 779
New Albany, OH 43054
1-(888)-391-LIFE

You can reach Faith Life Now Ministries on the Internet at www.faithlifenow.com.

# CONTENTS

INTRODUCTION......................................................05

Chapter One:
You can't take responsibility for someone else's life. .......09

Chapter Two:
You have to have courage to get anywhere in life. ...........31

Chapter Three:
There will be pressure. DON'T QUIT! ........................53

Chapter Four:
You need people and people need you. ..........................83

Chapter Five:
Ask for forgiveness and forgive. .....................................97

Chapter Six:
You can be financially free. ...........................................113

Conclusion................................................................133

Answer Key...............................................................135

# INTRODUCTION

*"The wise learn their lesson not by learning the hard way but by watching others learn the hard way."*

Learning is critical to your success in life. No matter your age, your title, or your net worth, you should always be actively looking to learn new things.

Why not learn them the easy way?

Because who really wants to learn by making mistakes;

through trial and error; or from bad, difficult, or unpleasant experiences?

*Not me.*

But I have. I've learned plenty of lessons in life the hard way.

And I want to help you so you don't have to.

You probably know some of my story: Years ago, my wife, Drenda, and I were in very serious debt. For nine long years, we lived hand-to-mouth, desperate, broke, and under extreme stress. One day I woke up in the morning and my face, tongue, and arms were all numb. I went to the doctor, and they couldn't find anything wrong.

After years of living in stress, fear, and under pressure, my body was shutting down.

I clearly remember the day I reached the end of my rope and I collapsed on my bed, desperately crying out to God. That was the day God said, "Take the time to learn how my Kingdom operates." And that was when everything changed.

Drenda and I began to learn how the Kingdom of God operates. We discovered real answers on how to release the Kingdom of God into our lives, and in less than three years from that day, we were completely out of debt.

We've been on a mission ever since to mentor others in all the things God taught us, as well as in the things we've learned on our own over the years in business, in marriage and family, and in life—too many times the hard way.

It's my hope that this little book can help YOU be "the wise," learning these six things by reading my stories rather than having to experience them or go through them yourself—that the things I learned the hard way, you won't have to.

Chapter One

# YOU CAN'T TAKE RESPONSIBILITY FOR SOMEONE ELSE'S LIFE.

Many years ago, before I was a pastor, I was a regional vice president for a company in Tulsa, Oklahoma.

I had a team of five full-time managers that worked for me. Every week, it was expected that we would make calls and set up appointments to fill in our schedules for the week.

But every week, those five managers would fail to fill their schedules with appointments.

I thought, *Okay, they're new at this. They just need a taste of how good business is and how easy it is to make money, and they'll jump in and get it done.*

So, I helped them. I made their calls for them, and I filled their weeks with appointments. For months, I sat in the office from 9:00 a.m. to 9:00 p.m. every Saturday making calls, filling up my schedule and theirs for the week.

And those five managers loved that. They were making more money than they had ever made in their lives. Every week, their schedules were booked up with appointments they hadn't had to make, and they didn't have to come in the office every Saturday to make calls. I was doing it all for them.

One day, the wife of one of the managers called me and told me her husband was at the bar getting drunk. She asked me to go to the bar and get him. I was shocked—this manager had told me and his wife that he was heading out to an appointment that I had set for him.

*That's it, Gary,* I thought. *You care more about this guy's family than he does. He won't even show up for an appointment that's already been set for him!*

That's when I stopped taking responsibility for those five managers. I realized I was robbing them of the pressure that would push them to make the calls on their own.

I had my own pressure and my own bills to pay. So, I would make the calls—the cold calls. (That's an industry term that means you call complete strangers and try to sell them something, or set up an appointment to sell them something.)

I'd make 90 cold calls a day, every day. I'd open the phone book and call strangers because I had bills to pay and a family to feed. Falsely, I assumed everyone would respond to pressure the way I had. My hope was that if my managers could just see how easy it was to make the sale once they were at a client's house, they would eagerly want to make the phone calls to set appointments. I discovered that was not the case.

And what happened when I stopped? They all quit.

That was a big eye-opener for me.

Learning not to take responsibility for the lives of other people has been one of the hardest lessons I've ever had to learn, and it's been a lesson I've had to learn several times, unfortunately.

When we first launched into ministry, we knew nothing about pastoring a church. We really believed that telling people about the goodness of God would be enough to win them for the Kingdom and make them successful.

We want everyone to experience life to its full potential. Drenda takes this to another level. Let's say you're eating with us in a restaurant, and she remarks how great something tastes. You innocently say that you have never had it before. The next thing you know, Drenda is sticking a spoonful in your face for you to try. We thought pastoring a church would be that way—if we could just get people to taste the goodness of God, they'd be hooked.

So, we began to pour into people and spend time with people and try to help them understand how good the Kingdom really is. We thought we could just drag them toward God and toward success. Our intentions were good, but the results were far from good.

It wasn't long before the counseling sessions we were doing with people got longer and more frequent, and we were paying more and more people's bills. In one stormy marriage counseling session, we even went so far as to recommend that the couple just needed some time to themselves and everything would be all right. To help them find some alone time, we paid for a Caribbean cruise and sent them on it. The result? They still ended up divorcing. The real eye-opener was that Drenda and I gave up the money that we'd been saving to take our own cruise.

No one could say we didn't care, but we slowly began to realize that our tactics were wrong. The only lives being changed were ours. We felt like we were carrying the weight of the world.

Then, we weren't carrying just our own family problems but the problems of 200+ people. We were trying to fix every business issue, financial concern, and marriage trouble, and it was too much.

I love God and I love the church, but living that way nearly drove Drenda and me out of ministry.

Around that time, a traveling pastor visited with us, and we explained how discouraged and worn out we were. After hearing all of our complaints, he laid the truth on the line. He said, "Gary, all you owe your people is an example and having fun. If you're not having fun, why would they want to join you?"

And I wasn't having fun. I was stressed out. Sure, Drenda and I had a great marriage and family. Our businesses were successful. Together, we *were* having fun. We were enjoying the Kingdom. But carrying burdens for everyone else was wearing us out.

I realized that because I had dealt with so much pressure for so many years, I had gotten in the habit of wanting to alleviate pressure for others. But I wasn't helping them.

If you know anything at all about raising chickens or how they hatch, you know that around the seventeenth day of incubation, the chicks will start to peep. The mother hen will hear the sound and will get more attentive toward her eggs. She'll stop turning them, something she's done several times a day since she laid them.

Here's what the mother hen *doesn't* do: She doesn't interpret the peeping as a cry for help.

It takes a few days for a chick to break out of the shell, but the peeps aren't their way of crying out, "Help me! Help me! I'm trapped, and I can't get out!"

No, what the chicks are really saying in the peeps is, "I'm getting stronger! I'm getting stronger!"

The stress and exertion of breaking through the shell is part of the process that strengthens the chicks. Just like cracking the shell open shuts down the growth process for the chick, taking responsibility for someone when they need to take responsibility for themselves prevents them from feeling the "struggle" that will drive them to change and succeed.

For example, as a pastor, many people come to me asking me to pray for their finances, which I have no problem doing. But I also ask questions because I want to see people fix their financial situations and find their God-designed purposes. I want to help them win in life.

So, I ask questions. And all too often, I come across situations where parents or grandparents are paying the mortgage payments, buying the groceries, and paying the utility bills for their *adult, perfectly able-bodied* children and grandchildren. Now I understand that at times anyone may need a little helping hand to bridge a negative circumstance. But someone who has a heart to help can very quickly become an enabler, and the one who is supposedly being helped can become entitled.

Why? Because it's really easy for people to get comfortable if you're frequently, or always, taking the load off of them.

Proverbs 20:4 says, "*A sluggard does not plow in season; so at harvest time he looks but finds nothing.*"

What's a sluggard? A sluggard is a lazy person, or a person who refuses to take personal responsibility.

So the lazy person doesn't plant or sow, and doesn't plow in season. But then they go looking for a harvest to be there when they need it—just like those five managers I had working for me years ago. They weren't sowing into the business. They weren't plowing the field looking for new customers. I was doing the sowing and the plowing for them. I was providing their harvest, until I wasn't. Then their entitled mind-set became offended and they left. In the end, whose fault was that? MINE! I killed the chicken in the egg! By removing pressure, I essentially guaranteed their failure when it was time for them to handle the weight of their own assignments. Instead of making those phones calls for them, I should have been coaching and mentoring them on a case-by-case basis all along, making them do all the work but encouraging and mentoring them through the process. After all, my confidence in making those calls had not come overnight but through years of hard work.

Here's the thing: There *are* people who genuinely need our help.

There are people who get in bad spots, suffer loss, or who just need some mentorship and coaching.

But, like me providing the appointments for those five managers for way too long, too often, the church will just continue to help someone without digging into the reasons why they *continue* to need help.

And if we're truly going to help people get better and win in life, we have to step back and help them identify where they need to grow, sow, and harvest for themselves.

Sometimes the very best thing is for a person to find himself or herself in a situation where they haven't taken the time or the responsibility they should have, and they're *hungry* (literally or figuratively.)

Proverbs 16:26 says, "*The laborer's appetite works for him; his hunger drives him on.*"

I know I'm not making friends when I say, *Let them get hungry*. After all, that wouldn't be Christian.

Years ago, Drenda and I knew a couple in our church who had hit tough times with job losses, and their house had gone into foreclosure. The sheriff's sale was scheduled. They needed $10,000 to bring the mortgage current. They had shared their situation with several people (usually anyone who would listen), including another couple who just so happened to have recently received an inheritance of hundreds of thousands of dollars.

So, the couple that had received the inheritance helped

them out and paid the $10,000 to bring the mortgage current. When the couple who had supplied the $10,000 told me what they had done, their comment was, "It seemed so wrong for us to have that much money and not do something for them." Was that a good reason to give them the $10,000? You see, this couple didn't know what I knew about the couple whose house was in foreclosure. As their pastor, I had been walking this out with them the whole time. I knew neither one of them had bothered to find jobs, and both the husband and the wife had been unemployed for months before the house foreclosure became inevitable. And it wasn't because there were no jobs out there, but they told me they couldn't find a job they really *liked*. Is that a valid reason to lose everything you own?

No one has a job where they love everything about it! Do you think I enjoyed making those 90 cold calls a day? No, I felt almost sick every morning before I made them.

Well, less than a year later, the couple was back in the same situation, and they lost the house that time. Giving them the $10,000 had just delayed the inevitable and had robbed the generous family of part of their inheritance. Taking the pressure off prematurely didn't help the ones under pressure.

Again, please understand my heart is always to be generous on every occasion as the Bible teaches us to be. But Jesus also said not to cast your pearls before the swine. Drenda and I have learned to ask questions and to help the person in need with a plan that they are responsible for and then to hold them accountable to the plan before we just throw money at the problem.

It's sad to say, but Drenda and I have so many stories like that, and it is unfortunate that we learned the hard way that we can't be the answer for people. No matter how much I hurt for a person, I can't take responsibility for their life. I can come alongside them and help, but I can't take false responsibility for where they are and how they got there. We must remember that the problem usually didn't happen overnight.

I can instruct them, and I can coach them, and I can tell them the truth in love, but nothing will change until they take personal responsibility.

And that doesn't just apply to financial situations.

Have you ever seen those reality shows that feature people who are several hundred pounds overweight? They're so overweight that they can't get out of their beds.

Who has enabled them? Who has been feeding them? Who has been afraid to tell them the truth? Who has refused to help them take personal responsibility?

Do you have friends or relatives that you're afraid to disappoint? Anytime they need something, you jump up and offer to fix it? They control you through their words, anger, or even their generosity?

Friend, you're not helping people by allowing them to continue in their dysfunction. You can be kind, gently instruct, love, and lead people to take personal responsibility.

Years ago, we had a family over for dinner, and the wife showed up with a bagged meal for her two children. When I asked her why she had brought their dinner, she explained that they were picky eaters, so she fixed them their own separate meals to bring to our home.

Notice I said *meals*. She had prepared TWO different meals to bring to our house for her children.

I was thinking, *Let them get hungry! You're creating monsters! This is easy to correct. Give them two or three days of not wanting to eat what you've prepared for the rest of the family, and I bet they change their minds.*

But she was continuing to enable those children—breaking their shells when they started peeping—weakening them, not strengthening them.

What will happen when they become adults and the whole world won't cater to them?

Paul wrote in 2 Thessalonians 3:6-10:

> *In the name of the Lord Jesus Christ, we command*

*you, brothers, to keep away from every brother who is idle and does not live according to the teaching you received from us.*

*For you yourselves know how you ought to follow our example. We were not idle when we were with you, nor did we eat anyone's food without paying for it. On the contrary, we worked night and day, laboring and toiling so that we would not be a burden to any of you.*

*We did this, not because we do not have the right to such help, but in order to make ourselves a model for you to follow. For even when we were with you, we gave you this rule: "If a man will not work, he shall not eat."*

Paul gave us a model: If a man will not work, he shall not eat. *Let him get hungry.*

But this isn't just about being hungry for food or other material earthly needs. This is also about being hungry for the Kingdom, for the goodness of God, for His great and precious promises, for real change.

It's human nature to avoid change until we face the facts. When life isn't working, many times, if not most of the time, there are spiritual issues that must be dealt with as well.

As I mentioned previously, Drenda and I were in serious debt for nine long, hard years. We so longed for freedom.

But until we realized we needed God's wisdom and His plan for our lives, we were not going anywhere. God wasn't the One that was causing our financial problems; we were because we would not heed His wisdom or seek out His truth. The bottom line is that we didn't have to go through those nine years of financial dysfunction; the truth was there all along if we would have only looked for it.

Now, understand what I'm saying. We're to help people in tough times. We're to help people as they're going *through* tough times.

We're to teach people. We're to mentor people. We're to demonstrate how things can and should be done. But we're not supposed to keep *doing for* them what they can and should be able to do for themselves at some point. There are some people who never seem to want to get *through*. Some people *want* to stay stuck.

Proverbs 12:15 says, "*The way of a fool seems right to him, but a wise man listens to advice.*"

Stop and think about it. Do you know anyone like that?

Is it you?

If so, it's time you took responsibility. It's time you got hungry—for change and for wisdom.

Drenda and I are millionaires today because we stopped and

examined our lives and asked God to help us, knowing that we had to change. It's kind of crazy to know how messed up we were then to now be doing TV all over the world helping people with their money. And God can do the same for you. No matter where you come from or how messed up your life might be at the moment, you can change and enjoy the good life that God has planned for you.

## BE "THE WISE."
### YOU DON'T HAVE TO DO THINGS THE HARD WAY.

*Go back through Chapter One and fill in the blanks from these important points.*

Taking responsibility for someone when they need to take responsibility for themselves prevents them from feeling the _____ that will drive them to change and succeed.

Someone who has a heart to help can very quickly become an _____, and the one who is supposedly being helped can become _____.

If we're truly going to help people get better and win in life, we have to step back and help them identify where they need to _____, _____, and _____ for themselves.

Sometimes the very best thing is for a person to find himself or herself in a situation where they haven't taken the _____ or the _____ they should have, and they're _____ (literally or figuratively.)

Proverbs 16:26 says, *"The laborer's appetite works _____ him; his _____ drives him on."*

Drenda and I have learned to _____ _____ and to help the person in need with a _____ that they are responsible for and then to hold them accountable to the plan before we just throw money at the problem.

You're not helping people by allowing them to continue in their _____. You can be kind, gently instruct, love, and lead people to _____ _____.

When life isn't working, many times, if not most of the time, there are _____ issues that must be dealt with as well.

## CONSIDER
### HAVE YOU BEEN DOING THIS THE HARD WAY?

Describe a time you tried to "help" someone change or do the right thing.

_____

_____

_____

Describe a time you found yourself doing things you didn't want to do or know you shouldn't have done in order to make someone else happy.

_____

_____

_____

_____

Really think about the people in your life. Do you have any friends or relatives (or both) that you're afraid to disappoint? Is there someone who you jump up to help anytime they call on you, or someone who controls you through their words, anger, or even their generosity?

_____

_____

_____

_____

_____

Galatians 6:2-5 says, *"Carry each other's burdens, and in this way you will fulfill the law of Christ. If anyone thinks he is something when he is nothing, he deceives himself. Each one should test his own actions. Then he can take pride in himself, without comparing himself to somebody else, for each one should carry his own load."*

How do you think this Scripture relates to "helping people in tough times … as they're going *through* tough times" as mentioned in this chapter?

_____

_____

_____

_____

_____

What do you think this Scripture means by "*each one should carry his own load*"?

_____

_____

_____

_____

In what ways do you recognize that taking responsibility for someone else's life has been wearing you out or hindering your life?

_____

_____

_____

_____

Write out Matthew 11:28-30:

_____

_____

_____

_____

Write out Proverbs 20:4:

_____

_____

_____

_____

What is *your* definition of a sluggard?

_____

_____

_____

Instead of removing pressure from someone else, what are some ways you might be able to help him or her handle the weight of their own situation?

_____

_____

_____

_____

Summarize 2 Thessalonians 3:6-10 in your own words:

_____

_____

_____

_____

Proverbs 12:15 says, "*The way of a fool seems right to him, but a wise man listens to advice.*" How are you about taking advice in your own life?

_____

_____

_____

_____

## CHALLENGE
### IT'S TIME TO TAKE ACTION.

Find someone who is modeling what you're looking for in your life—in business, marriage, parenting, leading, whatever—and schedule time with them in the next two weeks.

Be prepared to ask questions. Ask them why they do what they do, how they got started, where they came from, and what changed. Be coachable and humble as you listen.

Proverbs 13:20 says, *"He who walks with the wise grows wise, but a companion of fools suffers harm."*

# PRAYER

Father, You said in the Bible that Your
yoke is easy and Your burden is light.
Help me to release the burdens I am
carrying for other people in my life, like

_____

over to You and help me never to pick them
back up again. I ask that You reveal to me where
I am taking false responsibility for anyone else
and any areas of my own life in which I'm not
taking personal responsibility for myself, and
help me to change that. In Jesus's name, amen.

## Chapter Two

# YOU HAVE TO HAVE COURAGE TO GET ANYWHERE IN LIFE.

Years ago, I took my family camping in Colorado for the first time. We hiked through the national forest and found what we thought was a great spot to camp for the night.

The dark set in, and there we were, our family of seven, lying side-by-side in our tent ready to go to sleep and listening to sounds we'd never heard before coming from the woods.

That's when we saw it—a *giant animal shadow* on the side of the tent.

So, we all freaked out of course. We were in the middle of

the forest after all. There were bears and who knows what else out there. And all I had was a hatchet.

The shadow got *bigger.*

*Someone has to handle this,* I thought.

And because I'm the dad, of course, I had to be the one to pull it together and open the tent flap to see what was out there.

And there it was—*a little mouse* crawling up the tent pole.

Our lantern was outside on a picnic table near the tent, and the shadow the mouse cast had been distorted to look much larger than it really was.

Know this, friend: That's exactly how the devil operates. He presents false evidence—shadows, smoke screens, and setups—to scare you. He doesn't want you to know who you are, and he wants to steal every bit of courage from you that he can. Because he knows that as long as you're operating in fear, you'll stay zipped up in your tent, unable to discern the truth.

That's why 1 Peter 5:8 says, "*Be self-controlled and alert. Your enemy the devil prowls around like a roaring lion looking for someone to devour.*"

The enemy isn't looking to devour unbelievers. He already

has them. No, he's looking to devour believers.

He's looking to devour *you*, one bite—one lie, one deception—at a time.

But the enemy has already been defeated. So, as a believer, the real battle occurs in your *mind*. That's the only way he can gain entrance. That's why you have to take your thoughts captive. You have to draw the line. You have to stand your ground.

You have to have courage.

Here's the thing: Courage isn't the *absence* of fear. No, courage is actually defined as the mental or moral strength to venture, persevere, and withstand danger, fear, or difficulty. *Courage is moving forward in the face of fear.*

You have to have the courage to unzip the tent flap and discover the truth, or the enemy is going to hold you hostage in your tent, afraid of shadows, for your entire life.

Learning that I had to have courage was another lesson I learned the hard way. Sure, I pulled it together as a dad and husband and unzipped the tent flap to face whatever was casting the shadow on our tent that night in the woods, but I had lived most of my life before that hiding out in my proverbial tent.

Take a look at
this photograph.

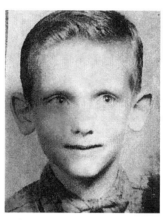

That's a picture of me in the second grade.

Now, you may have said, "Awww," because we tend to do that when we see childhood photos of people we know, but take another look.

Do you see my ears? They stuck straight out. I was born with no cartilage in my ears, so they stuck out from the side of my head. And, boy, was I picked on for those ears.

*One bite at a time.*

I don't know if the first lie the enemy told me was about my ears, but it was the first of many tactics the enemy used to get me to decide that I wasn't going to care, that I wasn't going to play the game of life—to keep me shut up in my tent, afraid of my own shadow.

*One bite at a time.*

I was also overweight. And because I was insecure about the way I looked and not confident in myself, I was shy. *Painfully shy.* I didn't talk. In fact, I pretty much did whatever I could to avoid talking and to avoid people. *Yes, I'm a pastor and speaker, and I used to avoid people. I admit it.*

I talked so rarely that when one of my teachers in high school walked by me in the hallway and heard me talking to a friend, she stopped and said, "So, you CAN talk!"

It was really bad. I played football in junior high and high school—I was a starting player—and my sisters were cheerleaders. My mother would have parties after the games, and I would hide in my room. And I didn't just go through high school barely speaking to people, I also had really poor grades. I graduated with a *1.3 grade point average.* There was only *one* other guy who had a lower GPA than I did. I was definitely not voted most likely to succeed.

*One bite at a time.*

I had learned the best way to survive life was to withdraw. In fact, my goal was to just get done with school and live in the woods, away from people.

I had zipped up my proverbial tent and determined I was *never* coming out to face the shadows, let alone learn the truth.

God had to fix me. He had a specific purpose for my life,

and He wanted to help me get there. When I was 19 years old, God called me in a vision to preach—*to people*. So I *had* to change. After all, a preacher who is afraid of people would live a miserable, unproductive life. There was only one answer: I had to have courage. I had to move forward in the face of fear again and again and again. I had to keep moving forward to get where He wanted me to go. My future on the inside had to get bigger than the perceived fear on the outside.

The Bible is full of examples of courage. Joshua is one of my favorites. Moses had mentored Joshua to be a successful leader. Then, Moses died. Suddenly, Joshua was responsible for a huge nation of people and a wilderness journey.

Joshua could've easily looked at his situation and freaked out. He could've said, "You've got to be kidding me. I can't do this. I'm not qualified." He could've holed up in his tent, afraid to unzip the flap and face whatever was out there.

But he didn't. Instead, Joshua focused on the promises God had made him:

> *I will give you every place where you set your foot, as I promised Moses. Your territory will extend from the desert to Lebanon, and from the great river, the Euphrates—all the Hittite country—to the Great Sea on the west.*

> *No one will be able to stand up against you all the*

*days of your life. As I was with Moses, so I will be with you; I will never leave you nor forsake you.*

*Be strong and courageous, because you will lead these people to inherit the land I swore to their forefathers to give them. Be strong and very courageous. Be careful to obey all the law my servant Moses gave you; do not turn from it to the right or to the left, that you may be successful wherever you go.*

*Do not let this Book of the Law depart from your mouth; meditate on it day and night, so that you may be careful to do everything written in it. Then you will be prosperous and successful.*

*Have I not commanded you? Be strong and courageous. Do not be terrified; do not be discouraged, for the Lord your God will be with you wherever you go.*
—Joshua 1:3-9

It's pretty obvious what God was trying to get across to Joshua.

*Be strong and courageous.*

Just like Joshua, you have to have courage to go into new territory, and to lead people to someplace they've never been. Faith can take you to the edge, but it's courage that helps you take the leap.

And know this: Courage isn't a feeling. God mandated that Joshua be courageous. That means courage is a *choice*, a *decision* to move forward in the face of fear.

No matter how impossible the situation may look, God said He is with you. It doesn't matter how weak you feel or how afraid you are. God said He will never leave you nor forsake you. He always shows up.

You can be courageous not because of who *you* are, but because of who *God* is.

And thank God for that, because one of the first things God told me to do after He called me to preach was to go to college.

*College, God? I barely graduated from high school!*

Talk about courage. I had never even been outside of Ohio, and there I was driving in my little Fiat to Oklahoma to go to college. It was there that I met Drenda and took several more courageous steps toward the life God had for me, but I still had quite a ways to go.

After college, God told me to go into life insurance sales. That's a fantastic job for someone who is afraid to talk to people, right? I died at least a thousand deaths every week during those years I sold insurance. I'd lay in bed at night shaking in fear. It was the fight of my life.

But that was when things really began to change—when I finally started to unzip the tent flap of my life and discover the truth about myself. That's when God began to reveal all of the larger-than-life shadows for what they really were—*lies*.

I had believed the lies of the enemy for so long—that my looks defined me, that I was too shy and couldn't talk to people, that I wasn't good enough, that I had no potential, that I wasn't capable of success.

I had allowed the enemy to take one bite of me at a time, until he had nearly devoured the plans God had for my life and my future.

But God called me to be strong and courageous, so I had to confront the larger-than-life shadows—the lies, the insecurities, the inferiorities, and the intimidation. Then, I had to have the courage to confront the circumstances that were holding me back, like the debt we had accumulated and my past failures.

And, you know what? Having the courage to face what I thought were my weaknesses was an incredible lesson. Because, in the end, what I thought were weaknesses became my strengths. The financial failures we faced and my previous fear of people are now tools God uses to share the glory and goodness of His Kingdom around the world.

Just like me, you have to find out who you are, realize that you are uniquely and specially made by God for a purpose, that you are precious to Him, and that He loves you enough to lay down the life of His only Son for you. You have to unzip the tent flap and face the lies of the enemy. Call his bluff. You can't be passive. Tell him to shut up; and get about your business, and be courageous about it. You have to take your stand of authority in the place God created for you.

Like Dorothy in the *Wizard of Oz*—she had the red slippers on all along. She already had everything she needed to get home to Kansas. She just didn't know it. You already have everything you need.

I had a vision to preach when I was 19, but vision without courage is useless.

It's courage combined with faith for your God-inspired vision that releases the anointing of God.

I meet so many Christians who believe they should start businesses or make a leap, but they never engage or confront. They never take a step of courage. Or they get tired.

I've been there.

Many years ago, before I pastored, I was dealing with a tooth situation. I went to the dentist, and he loaded a needle with some Novocain to numb the pain.

The moment he injected it, I felt an odd jolt, and my mouth was instantly numb.

I asked the dentist about the jolt. He said, "Oh, I hit the nerve. Don't worry, though, it usually heals up about 80% of the time."

*Eighty percent of the time?!*

"What happens in the other 20%?" I asked him.

"Permanent paralysis," he said. "But it's not common."

Now, the Bible tells us that the shield of faith extinguishes all the flaming arrows of the evil one (Ephesians 6:16), but when you're tired or you have too many things going on, you may not be in faith.

And that's exactly the opportunity the enemy is looking for. In fact, Luke 4:13 tells us that after Jesus stood against the devil's temptations in the wilderness that the enemy left to wait for a more opportune time.

*A more opportune time.*

He caught me when I was tired. I didn't pull out my Bible. I didn't rebuke the enemy or cast down the report of the dentist. No, I went to a friend to ask him what he thought, if he'd ever heard of this happening. "It can't be a big deal, right?" I asked him.

"My uncle is paralyzed because that happened to him," my friend told me.

*One bite at a time.*

So, what did I do? I asked a second person, who told me her aunt was paralyzed from the same thing. I had never heard of this happening to anyone. Now, two people in a row knew someone who had the exact thing I was fearing happen to them. What were the odds?

*Paralyzed.*

The numbness wasn't going away, and I couldn't shake the thoughts.

On top of what the dentist and my two friends had said, when I lay down that night, I started thinking about how my father had had Bell's palsy a few years before, which is when you have paralysis in your face due to damage to a nerve. I felt a twinge in the bone below my ear and thought, *You're going to have Bell's palsy.*

*One bite at a time.*

I woke up the next morning with full-blown Bell's palsy. I couldn't close my eye or my mouth. My entire face was paralyzed. The doctors said, "Well, it usually heals up about 80% of the time."

Thankfully, I was smart enough to know what came next. I determined that was the end. We put index cards of Scriptures all over the house, and I just kept quoting those Scriptures every day. About five days later, the anointing came on me, and I knew I was healed. Within an hour, the paralysis was completely gone.

See, the enemy isn't interested in a fraction. He doesn't want just an inch or a mile; he wants your entire life.

He's going to keep coming. He won't back off. He'll just wait for a more opportune time.

Be strong and courageous.

Don't be held hostage. Unzip the tent flap and face the dangers, the fears, and the difficulties. Then, keep moving forward.

## BE "THE WISE."
### YOU DON'T HAVE TO DO THINGS THE HARD WAY.

*Go back through Chapter Two and fill in the blanks from these important points.*

The devil operates by presenting false _____ —shadows, smokescreens, and setups—to scare you. He doesn't want you to know who you are, and he wants to steal every bit of _____ from you that he can. Because he knows that as long as you're operating in _____, you'll stay zipped up in your tent, unable to discern the truth.

The enemy isn't looking to devour unbelievers. He already has them. No, he's looking to devour believers. He's looking to devour _____, one bite—one _____, one _____—at a time.

But the enemy has already been defeated. So, as a believer, the real battle occurs in your _____.

Courage isn't the _____ of fear. No, courage is actually defined as the mental or moral strength to venture, persevere, and withstand danger, fear, or difficulty. Courage is _____ _____ in the face of fear.

Just like Joshua, you have to have _____ to go into new territory, and to lead people to someplace they've never been. _____ can take you to the edge, but it's _____ that helps you take the leap.

Courage is a _____, a decision to move forward in the face of fear.

You can be courageous not because of who you are, but because of who _____ is.

It's courage combined with _____ for your God-inspired _____ that releases the _____ of God.

The enemy isn't interested in a fraction. He doesn't just want an inch or a mile; he wants your _____ _____.

## CONSIDER
### HAVE YOU BEEN DOING
### THIS THE HARD WAY?

Describe a time you let fear get the best of you.

Describe a time you know the enemy set up something to scare you and steal your courage, and what happened.

Write out 1 Peter 5:8:

In what ways have you "moved forward in the face of fear" in your life?

_____

_____

_____

_____

Think about what one of your old photographs shows about who you were. How have you changed since that photo was taken?

_____

_____

_____

What have you withdrawn from in your life because you believed a lie or thought it was what you had to do to survive?

_____

_____

_____

The Bible is full of examples of courage. This chapter focuses on Joshua. What did God emphasize to Joshua (in Joshua 1:3-9)?

_____

_____

_____

Who is someone else in the Bible who demonstrated courage?

Before reading this chapter, did you view courage as a choice? If not, how does learning that change things for you?

What larger-than-life shadows—lies, insecurities, inferiorities, or intimidations—do you recognize you need to confront in your life?

Write out Ephesians 6:16:

_____

_____

_____

_____

When you're facing down fear in a situation, who are you most likely to turn to—God, a family member, a friend? Should you change that?

_____

_____

_____

Write out Deuteronomy 31:8:

_____

_____

_____

Write out Isaiah 43:1:

_____

_____

_____

## CHALLENGE
### IT'S TIME TO TAKE ACTION.

Determine TODAY that you'll no longer be held hostage by fear, and make the decision to unzip the "tent flap" and face the dangers, the fears, and the difficulties in your life.

Write out Scriptures that specifically fight fear and encourage you to be strong and courageous on index cards or sticky notes and put them all over your house, in your car, and at work. Keep speaking them every day until you see evidence of change in your life.

Here are a few to help get you started:

- Psalm 18:2 – *"The Lord is my rock, my fortress and my deliverer; my God is my rock, in whom I take refuge. He is my shield and the horn of my salvation, my stronghold."*

- Psalm 56:3 – *"When I am afraid, I will trust in you."*

- Philippians 4:6-7 – *"Do not be anxious about anything, but in everything, by prayer and petition, with thanksgiving, present your requests to God. And the peace of God, which transcends all understanding, will guard your hearts and your minds in Christ Jesus."*

- John 14:27 – *"Peace I leave with you; my peace I give you. I do not give to you as the world gives. Do not let your hearts be troubled and do not be afraid."*

- 2 Timothy 1:7 – *"For God did not give us a spirit of timidity, but a spirit of power, of love and of self-discipline."*

# PRAYER

Father, help me not to be distracted and to stay alert to the tactics of the enemy in my life. Give me the courage to unzip the tent flap in my life, confront the lies of the enemy, and discover the truth about myself. Use what I see right now as my weaknesses as tools to share the glory and goodness of Your Kingdom with the world. In Jesus's name, amen.

## Chapter Three

# THERE WILL BE PRESSURE. DON'T QUIT!

*I'm stressed out.*

*There's too much pressure.*

*This is overwhelming.*

*I can't do this.*

Sound familiar?

As Christians, I think we get confused sometimes. We look for things to be easy. But God never said things would be *easy*; He just said all things are *possible* (Matthew 19:26).

You have an enemy, after all, and he isn't going to give up territory just because you showed up. In fact, he's going to try to challenge you every single step of the way. Because he would like nothing better than to have you quit everything good and everything righteous in your life. And your flesh plays right along. Your flesh wants you to sit around and drink lemonade. It doesn't want to deal with pressure. It wants to escape hard things. It lives for quitting—for five o'clock, for Friday night, for vacation, and for retirement.

Our culture is set up to cater to our flesh too. You can microwave your dinner, make a call for delivery, or hit a drive-through and have whatever you want "your way." You can watch what you want, buy what you want, and reach who you want all in just seconds with just the click of a button or two. We've gotten so used to near-instant results that when we don't get them, we get disillusioned and want to quit. But that's the world's system, not God's.

God has a system in place to change us, mature us, and train us, and most of it won't ever be comfortable or easy or instant.

When God called me to preach and told me to go to college, then to do insurance sales, it wasn't comfortable or easy or instant. You would think I would've learned through those experiences that launching out on a God-idea, no matter how small or how big, would mean I'd face pressure. But I still had plenty of lessons to learn.

*O you foolish and thoughtless and superficial Galatians, who has bewitched you [that you would act like this], to whom—right before your very eyes—Jesus Christ was publicly portrayed as crucified [in the gospel message]?*

*This is all I want to ask of you: did you receive the [Holy] Spirit as the result of obeying [the requirements of] the Law, or was it the result of hearing [the message of salvation and] with faith [believing it]?*

*Are you so foolish and senseless? Having begun [your new life by faith] with the Spirit, are you now being perfected and reaching spiritual maturity by the flesh [that is, by your own works and efforts to keep the Law]?*

*Have you suffered so many things and experienced so much all for nothing—if indeed it was all for nothing? So then, does He who supplies you with His [marvelous Holy] Spirit and works miracles among you, do it as a result of the works of the Law [which you perform], or because you [believe confidently in the message which you] heard with faith?*

—Galatians 3:1-5 (AMP)

That right there is the very first message God gave me to preach when we launched Faith Life Church more than 22 years ago. I still have my notes.

At first, I didn't understand why God wanted me to share that message. But then I understood that He was talking to me and clearly saying, "Gary, it isn't about you. You're launching into a venture that is not about you and never will be about you. You are to keep your eyes on Me. I am your strength, and you'll be foolish and senseless to ever think you have the ability to do this in your own strength."

Wow. Encouraging, right?

It was. Because here's the thing: Most of us launch out into things in faith, having heard from God, but then we somehow end up in places where we're trying to do it in our own strength—where we're trying to carry out ourselves what the Spirit of God started. I learned that the hard way.

For three years, we were invited to have our church operate out of the building of a local Christian radio station for free. *Completely free.* Free is almost always good.

And we kept growing until we were out of space at the radio station. We were bursting at the seams and needed to find a new facility as quickly as possible. We didn't want to go out of the city, but real estate in the area was scarce at the time.

Drenda came to me and said, "I found the only building that is available in New Albany, but I think it will work out great. It's $4,000 a month."

*Wait. What? Did you just say $4,000 a month?*

*The radio station space is free! The rent on our farmhouse is only $300 a month! Our church only has about 130 people! We'll have to buy chairs, a sound system, and all the things....*

Are you getting this?

I just couldn't wrap my head around paying $4,000 a month. Plus, we had to sign a lease for three years or five years. It was too much, and I refused to even pray about it.

But Drenda got me. It came close to the deadline, and she walked into my office and asked me if I had decided about the building. I told her I hadn't.

"Have you prayed about this?" she asked.

*Sigh.*

"No," I told her as she gave me that look she gives me when she isn't happy. The reality was that I hadn't prayed about it *at all* because, frankly, I was afraid God was going to say yes.

"Well, I'm leaving you alone in your office to pray about this because we need an answer by tomorrow morning!" she said. Then she closed the door and left me alone to pray.

Well, I prayed for about two minutes, and the Holy Spirit very clearly said that we were supposed to rent the warehouse. And we did, and it worked out great.

But I almost missed that opportunity. I almost missed out on where God was trying to take the church. And why? Because I had forgotten what He had taught *me* through that very first message I preached from Galatians 3. I faced pressure and I evaluated the possibilities for the future of the church based on my own strengths (or weaknesses), my own history, and my own perception, which only made me want to quit pushing forward.

**Know this: If you're going to do anything God wants you to do in your life, you will absolutely face pressure and uncomfortable, tough decisions.**

You don't have to learn that the hard way. I already did that for you. Start now knowing that there are going to be things that don't look possible, because they're not without God.

We began to look for land almost immediately after we started renting the warehouse, because we knew we couldn't stay there permanently. The building was falling apart. It didn't testify of God's goodness, and we were also quickly outgrowing it. So, we bought some land and paid it off.

Things appeared to be going great, but something was wrong.

Now, let me be clear that up until that point in my life, I

had always been in sales. I had never written job descriptions or created organizational charts. Yes, I had a business with hundreds of salespeople, but they were all commission-based employees, which pretty much meant they managed themselves.

The church was different. I had just five employees, but things were out of whack. Because I didn't know what I was doing and I hadn't trained them, my employees ended up managing me.

I had no clue what a leader was supposed to do. I thought leaders were supposed to give all the answers. So, that's what I did—I answered *every single question*. It was unintentional micromanaging. *I* decided if we were having hot dogs or hamburgers at the church picnic. *I* decided what toppings. *I* made *all* of the decisions.

It was chaos, and I was completely exhausted.

I felt completely ineffective.

I was so discouraged that I wanted to quit pastoring.

Here we had bought and paid for this beautiful land to build our new church building on, but in the three years we owned it, I hadn't once driven to it, let alone walked it to pray over it or get a vision for what God wanted to do there. I just couldn't imagine the chaos that I was living being multiplied. It was too much.

I was nearing rock bottom.

Drenda had heard of this gentleman by the name of Dr. Dean Radtke, a professional performance coach, and he just so happened to be in town for a leadership conference right around that time. We attended, and I was completely overwhelmed by the amount of material he shared. We asked him to meet us privately after the conference, and he did.

Just as I began to explain my situation, Dean said, "Gary, it's going to get worse. You have to get better."

I can imagine the look on my face as I thought, *How can it possibly get any worse? I'm already miserable!*

But Dean's coaching and his systems changed our lives. We needed better processes in place to help us more effectively lead our growing ministry and businesses, and he helped us get there.

But we had to walk it out. And so will you.

But you can learn the easy way what I had to learn the hard way—that there will be pressure when you launch out on a God-idea, but pressure isn't your enemy. Pressure usually leads to frustration, and frustration is the breeding ground of change.

Don't quit just when it gets uncomfortable or hard. Because when you push forward through the pressure, you'll find your victory, and your future, on the other side.

The 330 people who made up our warehouse church decided we were going to build a building, and that building was going to cost millions of dollars. Those 330 people raised $2.5 million of the $5.3 million it took to build the initial structure. The sound equipment, chairs, and everything in the building cost us another $1 million.

Now, remember, I freaked out about the $4,000 a month lease payment at the warehouse. But in reality, that was never hard to pay. God was faithful. He was faithful for the $4,000. He would be faithful with the new building.

See, in God's Kingdom, it just gets bigger. The zeros just get added on. You build upon history. You step out. You have bigger faith.

Look at Matthew 25. Jesus is telling the parable of the talents.

> *Again, it will be like a man going on a journey, who called his servants and entrusted his property to them. To one he gave five talents of money, to another two talents, and to another one talent, each according to his ability. Then he went on his journey.*
> —Matthew 25:14-15

Do you see that? The master gave to each of his servants according to their ability. This is a key part of the story.

> *The man who had received the five talents went at once and put his money to work and gained five more. So also, the one with the two talents gained two more.*
>
> *But the man who had received the one talent went off, dug a hole in the ground and hid his master's money.*
>
> *After a long time the master of those servants returned and settled accounts with them. The man who had received the five talents brought the other five. "Master," he said, "you entrusted me with five talents. See, I have gained five more."*
>
> *His master replied, "Well done, good and faithful servant! You have been faithful with a few things; I will put you in charge of many things. Come and share your master's happiness!"*
>
> *The man with the two talents also came. "Master," he said, "you entrusted me with two talents; see, I have gained two more."*
>
> *His master replied, "Well done, good and faithful servant! You have been faithful with a few things; I will put you in charge of many things. Come and share your master's happiness!"*

*Then the man who had received the one talent came. "Master," he said, "I knew that you are a hard man, harvesting where you have not sown and gathering where you have not scattered seed. So I was afraid and went out and hid your talent in the ground. See, here is what belongs to you."*

*His master replied, "You wicked, lazy servant! So you knew that I harvest where I have not sown and gather where I have not scattered seed? Well then, you should have put my money on deposit with the bankers, so that when I returned I would have received it back with interest. Take the talent from him and give it to the one who has the ten talents."*

*For everyone who has will be given more, and he will have an abundance. Whoever does not have, even what he has will be taken from him. And throw that worthless servant outside, into the darkness, where there will be weeping and gnashing of teeth.*

—Matthew 25:16-30

Let's examine what we see in this story because it's a key principle that, if you embrace it, will set you up on the course for major increase.

In the story we see that there are three guys working for the master. The master plans to go out of town, so he gives each of them an assignment that is equal to their ability and their proven capacity to manage and handle responsibility.

So, when the master returns, the five-talent guy comes back to the master with five more than he started with. He's no longer a five-talent guy because he's doubled his capacity.

Now, notice that the story doesn't tell us that the master gave the five-talent guy a five-talent assignment. It just says he gave him five talents according to his ability. So, really, the master gave the five-talent guy a ten-talent assignment—one that would pull on him—because he knew that servant had the ability to create solutions. He had proven in the past that he could handle responsibility and deal with the pressure to get to the five-talent level. Now, the master expected his capacity to enlarge even more as he dealt with the pressure and allowed himself to be stretched.

But the five-talent guy had a choice on how he would respond to the pressure. He could react in fear:

> *There's too much pressure.*

> *I'm already maxed out.*

> *I don't know how to do this.*

Those are pretty normal responses, actually. Because, for most of us, the processes we currently operate by limit our capacity for increase. Just like my broken processes with just five employees were limiting me and would never, ever work for a larger church with more employees. In order to increase anything in your life, you have to allow the Holy Spirit to help you change or correct your processes, how you do things.

Think of Subway, for example. At the time of printing, Subway has nearly 45,000 stores in more than 100 countries, all because someone decided a long time ago that they could make a sandwich that other people would want to eat.

But Subway started out at just one location with just a few employees making a few sandwiches a day. Then, someone decided they could duplicate that model, and they could take over the world with sub sandwiches.

Look back at Matthew 25:21:

> *His master replied, "Well done, good and faithful servant! You have been faithful with a few things; I will put you in charge of many things. Come and share your master's happiness!"*

Notice that it doesn't say, "You've been faithful with *everything*," or "You've been faithful with *many* things." No, the master said, "You've been faithful with a *few* things; I will put you in charge of *many* things."

*That's called stretching.*

The master was wise enough to know he needed to stretch the servant, because the servant had no idea of his capabilities. He needed to give him an assignment that would pull on his creativity and let him come to conclusions and bring solutions.

Think of it like a balloon. A balloon only has the capacity to hold more air if it's blown up—if it's *stretched*.

*We all need to be stretched.*

That's part of God's process. But that's also when most people want to quit. Because the survival world we all grew up in has taught us that it's safer if we just don't engage. It's better if we don't accept the challenge. After all, we've never done anything like that before, so let's just stay where we are and play it safe.

But God wants you to go for it.

As we were making plans to build the new church building, God told me to start doing television.

*Television, God? I mean, come on. We have stuff to do here. We're taking all of the money coming in to build the new building. Could you have worse timing? Can't this wait until next year? We're already maxed out. I can show you the calendar.*

But God doesn't get maxed out, and He looks at you from

the same perspective.

So God lined things up for us to do television. But then we hit an obstacle—it would cost $250,000 to start a television ministry. *More pressure.* Keep in mind that our people were already committing their funds to build the new church building. We were draining our bank account each week to pay contractors, and Drenda and I had personally committed a couple hundred thousand dollars to the new building. We didn't have $250,000 to start TV.

During that time, I was speaking at churches, teaching out of my series, *The Now Revolution.* In an offering at one of the churches, there was a gold coin. It was the first real gold coin I had ever held. God told me He had that gold coin placed in the offering to remind me and assure me that, as He had told Peter where the money was (in the fish's mouth in Matthew 17), He would tell me where the money was that I needed for the TV ministry.

So I held onto that gold coin. I held it and I prayed, and prayed, and prayed some more. Because in the natural, it just wasn't possible for us to come up with the money. I was feeling the pressure. It was uncharted territory. I didn't want to jump in there and risk everything. After all, I was a pastor who preached about fixing your money thing.

But we said yes to God, and we launched television. Our airtime cost around $9,000 a month back then. It was a lot of money. But God *always* keeps His promises, and that first year, through various circumstances, God brought in all the money we needed.

Then came the second year.

We were in the middle of everything. The building was going up, and God had directed us to increase our airtime. I was feeling the pressure. It was going to cost $20,000 a month.

*God, you know a month is only 30 days, right? We have millions we need here.*

But He was trying to get *me* to understand something, not the other way around.

God brings more opportunities when we say yes.

The pressure of those opportunities can easily make us say no, but then we'll quit advancing.

It wasn't long before our television costs had increased to about $50,000 a month. *Remember when I was freaking out about a $4,000 a month rent payment?*

It was intense. I couldn't see how we could keep paying for television. My mind just couldn't see where the money was going to come from.

One day I was really feeling sorry for myself. I told God it wasn't fair. I told God it was too much. I was having a real pity party.

"Is the bill due now?" God asked me.

"No," I answered.

"Shut up. It'll be here," He said.

You would think God telling me to shut up would've been enough, right? Well, it wasn't. That's when I went to a friend's conference in Atlanta. I was trying to escape. I was trying to clear my head. I was trying to get some encouragement.

No one knew I would be at the conference, so I was stunned when a lady came running up to me and said, "You're here!"

She was beyond excited as she explained how God had spoken to her in prayer that morning and told her to do something. She said she didn't know what it meant, but that I would.

She dug around in her purse and said, "I'm supposed to give you this."

In her hand was a *quarter wrapped in gold foil.*

I was flabbergasted.

I knew right then that God was trying to get me to *remember*. I knew the principles. I had let the pressure get to me. I just had to go back and remember what God had said.

*Galatians 3, Gary. Get your eyes off of yourself. In your own strength, your own power, you can't do this.*

Of course, I repented right there and got myself back in alignment with what God was saying. And the money came in. And we kept growing. Now, our television bill is several hundred thousand dollars a month, and I can sleep at night. I don't freak out. Why? My perspective changed. I've learned to allow God's process of pressure to enlarge my capacity.

I can keep going with story after story of all the amazing things God has done in my life, but the point is if you're going to do anything great in your life with God, there will be pressure.

The harvest will *always* be too big for you and your capacity. You have to work with God, and you have to let Him stretch you.

Don't quit.

Say yes to the process and trust God to give you the strength you need and the answers you could never come up with on your own.

> *Do you not know? Have you not heard? The Lord is the everlasting God, the Creator of the ends of the earth. He will not grow tired or weary, and his understanding no one can fathom.*
>
> *He gives strength to the weary and increases the power of the weak.*
>
> *Even youths grow tired and weary, and young men stumble and fall; but those who hope in the Lord will renew their strength. They will soar on wings like eagles; they will run and not grow weary, they will walk and not be faint.*
>
> —Isaiah 40:28-31

## BE "THE WISE."
## YOU DON'T HAVE TO DO THINGS THE HARD WAY.

*Go back through Chapter Three and fill in the blanks from these important points.*

God never said things would be _____; He just said all things are possible.

God has a system in place to _____ us, _____ us, and _____ us, and most of it won't be comfortable or easy or instant.

Most of us launch out into things in _____, having heard from God, but then we somehow end up in places where we're trying to do it in our own _____.

If you're going to do anything God wants you to do in your life, you will absolutely face _____ and uncomfortable, tough _____.

Start now knowing that there are going to be things that don't look possible, because they're not _____ _____.

There will be _____ when you launch out on a God-idea, but pressure isn't your enemy. Pressure usually leads to _____, and frustration is the breeding ground of _____.

When you push forward through the pressure, you'll find your _____, and your _____, on the other side.

In God's Kingdom, it just gets _____.

For most of us, the _____ we currently operate by limit our _____ for increase.

In order to increase anything in your life, you have to allow the Holy Spirit to help you _____ or _____ your _____, how you do things.

We all need to be _____.

God doesn't get _____ _____, and He looks at you from the same perspective.

God brings more opportunities when we _____ _____.

The pressure of those opportunities can easily make us say no, but then we'll quit _____.

The _____ will *always* be too big for you and your _____. You have to work with God, and you have to let Him _____ you.

## CONSIDER
### HAVE YOU BEEN DOING THIS THE HARD WAY?

List three things in your life you thought would be easier than they have been:

1. _____

2. _____

3. _____

Are you living your life right now looking forward to quitting—for five o'clock, for Friday night, for vacation, or for retirement? Why, or why not?

_____

_____

_____

_____

In what areas of your life have you been trying to do things in your own strength?

_____

_____

_____

_____

What looks impossible to you in your life right now?

_____

_____

_____

_____

Write out Matthew 19:26:

_____

_____

_____

_____

Write out Galatians 3:1-5 from a version other than the Amplified Bible:

_____

_____

_____

_____

What opportunities do you think you've missed because you caved under pressure or evaluated the possibilities based on your own strengths, weaknesses, history, or perception?

_____

_____

_____

_____

What important keys about increase did you learn from the parable of the talents from Matthew 25:14-30?

_____

_____

_____

_____

Have you proven in the past that you can handle responsibility and deal with the pressure to get to your next level? If so, how? If not, why?

_____

_____

_____

_____

_____

List three "processes" in your life right now that you know need to be changed or corrected:

1. _____

   _____

2. _____

   _____

3. _____

   _____


List three areas of your life where you believe God wants to stretch you or you know you need to be stretched:

1. _____

   _____

2. _____

   _____

3. _____

   _____

Write out Isaiah 40:28-31:

_____

_____

_____

_____

## CHALLENGE
### IT'S TIME TO TAKE ACTION.

Luke 16:10-12 says, *"Whoever can be trusted with very little can also be trusted with much, and whoever is dishonest with very little will also be dishonest with much. So if you have not been trustworthy in handling worldly wealth, who will trust you with true riches? And if you have not been trustworthy with someone else's property, who will give you property of your own?"*

Take a long, hard look at your life right now. Are you being faithful in the little things? Are you steadfast with how you're taking care of your family, your house, and your car? When was the last time you had a family night, dusted your furniture, or cleaned the old French fries out from between your car seats?

How faithful are you in following through, returning phone calls, honoring your word, or keeping your promises?

If you're believing God for big things, you must be willing to address the little areas you're not trustworthy in.

List three "little things" in your life you know you need to be more faithful in, and take action to be more trustworthy in them immediately:

1. _____

_____

2. _____

_____

3. _____

_____

# PRAYER

Father, I pray for supernatural strength from You to face all of the pressures in my life. I'm believing You for greater things in my life, and I know You have a great system in place to change me, mature me, and train me. I thank You for helping me to be faithful in the little things as well as the big things You've called me to. I praise You for all of the things in my life that don't look possible, like

_____,

because they're NOT possible without YOU! I put my trust in You—the One who never fails! Thank You in advance for all the ways You are moving in my life. In Jesus's name, amen.

## Chapter Four

# YOU NEED PEOPLE AND PEOPLE NEED YOU.

You can't do it alone.

But a lot of people have a lot of issues, right? I get it. After all, if you read lesson #2 that I learned the hard way, you know I had zero interest in being around people as a teen. My plan was to graduate from high school and live in the woods, away from people.

Growing up, I didn't really have a model for healthy relationships. I had a great family, but relationships weren't part of our family's life. My dad was a good man, but he wasn't saved until he was 80 years old. It was one of the greatest transformations I've ever seen in my life. But, up until that point, I had never seen him hug or kiss my mother or tell her he loved her. I was 55 years old the first time he told me he loved me.

So, I didn't have a clue about how to build relationships. But, of course, God called me to preach, so we had a problem. *I was the problem.* God was calling me to help people, but I didn't *like* people. Something had to change, and it wasn't going to be God.

Running away, backing up, hiding out, or trying to escape weren't options. They're never the answer. Engaging is.

And engage I did. God sent me Drenda, the most beautiful and wonderful girl I had ever seen. But, man, did I have a lot to learn. I hadn't been mentored to love my wife or lead a family. I admit I was almost clueless when it came to marriage and being a father.

Not only that, but I was coming out of years of insecurity from high school with a 1.3 grade point average, as you read in Chapter Two.

Drenda, on the other hand, *was* actually voted most likely to succeed. She was a great leader, president of her high school class of 500+, editor of the school paper, valedictorian, a great writer ... I could go on and on.

It didn't require a counselor to predict there would be some conflict when we got married.

For the first few years of our marriage, her energy and vision intimidated me. I was insecure, so instead of celebrating her giftings and her uniqueness, I saw them as threats.

*You're probably starting to see how this was a lesson I learned the hard way.*

Stick with me here for a few minutes while I talk about marriage, because that was my first training ground for relationships.

Proverbs 18:22 says, "*He who finds a wife finds what is good and receives favor from the Lord.*"

Favor is help. In fact, the definition in the dictionary includes the words backing, support, and assistance. It's a *gift*.

Drenda was a gift. God knew I really needed her and her giftings.

But I had to learn more about her and how to love her the way she needed to be loved. I had to learn that she is *for* me and not against me. I had to learn how to work in partnership with her. Those first years of marriage were a training ground for all that God wanted to do in my life.

Drenda and I have a fantastic marriage. She likes to share things in her conference speaking engagements like how I cook breakfast for her every day and serve her in bed, but I make sure I share how it definitely wasn't always that way.

There were plenty of times in the early years of our marriage that she would tell me that she didn't think I loved her. I'd respond with, "I just told you I love you." But she'd point out how I didn't take the trash out, or change the light bulbs, or concern myself with pretty much anything that was going on in her world.

Jesus said if we love Him, we will keep His commandments (John 14:15).

Love requires action.

If you really love Jesus, you're going to do what He says. If you really love your spouse, you're going to be concerned about his or her world and show it.

Unfortunately, I had to learn this lesson the hard way and more than once. God had to humble me many times.

*You don't like how she's acting, Gary?* God asked me one day when I was complaining in prayer about how snappy and clearly frustrated Drenda was with me.

*No, I don't.* I replied. *And I want you to do something about it.*

*It's your fault,* God said. *It's ALL your fault she's acting this way. She is reflecting how you treat her. If you want to see Drenda change, you need to love her and give to her without thinking of anything in return; love her without looking for any kind of response. You just begin to sow toward her.*

Ephesians 5:25-28 say,

> *Husbands, love your wives, just as Christ loved the church and gave himself up for her to make her holy, cleansing her by the washing with water through the word, and to present her to himself as a radiant church, without stain or wrinkle or any other blemish, but holy and blameless. In this same way, husbands ought to love their wives as their own bodies. He who loves his wife loves himself.*

This is a key principle. The Bible tells us husbands to love our wives as Christ loved the church. He gave Himself up for her to make her holy. He took the responsibility to wash her and present her to Himself as a radiant church, without stain, wrinkle, or any other blemish.

But I wasn't doing that.

In fact, back in those days when God was training me, I would sometimes casually, in a conversation with the guys, not honor my wife or uphold her. I was never abusive or malicious, but I didn't always speak about her with respect. And God told me to stop doing that. He said, *From now on, Gary, whenever you do that, you will call every single person who was in the room and apologize to them.*

So, there I was shortly after He told me that calling 27 people and apologizing for what I said and for not honoring my wife.

This happened three times before I really started paying attention to what I said casually in conversation about my wife.

God had to train me.

He knew that if I couldn't learn how to love my own wife and my own family, I would never be able to love other people and represent Him well to my church.

I think about how far I've come when I watch our old home movies. There's one in particular that is always hard to watch and is seared in my memory because it shows how much God had to train me in the area of relationships.

The kids were in the yard playing when I pulled in the driveway. They screamed, "Daddy's here!" and came running up and hugged my legs.

But, in the video, I didn't even look at them. I didn't say hello. I didn't say their names. I just walked into the house without saying a word to them.

It's heartbreaking and horrible and always makes me cry.

I was under such an incredible weight of financial stress back then. I was the husband and dad who lived his life barking orders, who was always distant and distracted, instead of building relationships with my wife and children.

God had to train me and change me.

He didn't want me to do life alone. He wasn't going to let me run away and hide in the woods. He had a plan for my life that was greater than anything I could imagine—a plan that involved people. I couldn't do it alone.

God doesn't want you to do life alone. He created you for relationship, with Him and with others. He knows how to help you have happy and healthy relationships. Let him train you and change you, because you need people, and people need you.

## BE "THE WISE."
### YOU DON'T HAVE TO DO THINGS THE HARD WAY.

*Go back through Chapter Four and fill in the blanks from these important points.*

Running away, backing up, hiding out, or trying to escape weren't options. They're never the answer. _____ is.

Love requires _____.

If you really love Jesus, you're going to _____ what He says. If you really love your spouse, you're going to be concerned about his or her world and _____ it.

You need _____, and people need _____.

God doesn't want you to do life alone. He created you for _____, with Him and with others.

Who are your models for healthy relationships?

Do you really act like you "like" people? Why or why not?

Who do you have conflict with in your life? Why?

What relationships in your life would you consider God's "training ground for relationships" for you?

_____

_____

_____

_____

Is there anyone in your life who intimidates you or who you see as a threat? If so, what specifically about them intimidates you or threatens you?

_____

_____

_____

_____

Write out John 14:15:

_____

_____

_____

_____

In what ways do you demonstrate love to the people around you?

_____

_____

_____

Describe how God has had to train you in one of your relationships:

_____

_____

_____

_____

What stresses or burdens have you been carrying that are negatively affecting your relationships?

_____

_____

_____

_____

How has God used someone else in your life?

_____

_____

_____

_____

## CHALLENGE
### IT'S TIME TO TAKE ACTION.

List three people who have made a difference in your life:

1. ......................................................................................................

2. ......................................................................................................

3. ......................................................................................................

Thank them somehow this week. Write them a note, send them a text, get them some flowers, etc. Let them know how they've impacted your life.

# PRAYER

Father, I know You created me for relationship
with You and with others. I thank You
for the people You've put in my life, like

_____.

He/she is a gift to me, and You knew I really
needed him/her and his/her giftings. I praise
You for training me in relationships so I can be
about Your business in the earth realm—the
people business. Help me to love my family
well, to be open to let the Holy Spirit do His
work, to show Your love everywhere I go, and
to be obedient when You tell me to speak up. In
Jesus's name, amen.

Chapter Five

# ASK FOR FORGIVENESS AND FORGIVE.

It was Father's Day, and I was frustrated.

We were visiting Drenda's parents and going to church with them. We were running behind, and my son Tom, who was about four years old at the time, couldn't find his shoes.

*Not again. We don't have time for this.*

Tom was always losing his shoes. This was the last straw. A four-year-old should know better, right?

So, I talked to Tom, and I was harsh. I didn't use bad language, but I did say things like, *I can't believe you always* and *Why can't you*, and my words and actions made Tom cry. He cried *hard*.

His big sister found his shoes; and we loaded into our van to get to church, and he was in the backseat still crying. I was thinking it was good for him. He needed to learn a lesson.

So, he went into the kids' area crying, and I went into the adult area to learn about how to be a good father without us saying a word to each other.

*Ouch.* The Holy Spirit completely *nailed* me as the pastor taught from God's Word on what it meant to be a father. The Holy Spirit whispered to me, "Gary, you have a problem. You have to deal with this."

Then, I was the one crying. And I was the first one at the altar. I knew I needed help. I knew I needed God to teach me how to be a good father.

Service ended, and we were waiting for the children to be released. I spotted Tom right away. He was jumping up and down in the crowd of kids.

*He was looking for me.*

When he spotted me, his little face just lit up, and he ran directly to me and hugged my leg and started crying again.

Now, this is where I always fall apart. Because even after all of these years, it's still a painful reminder of the way I was.

Tom looked up at me and said, "Daddy, I'm sorry I lost my shoes."

The little guy had sat through the whole church service thinking there was something wrong with him; that his daddy was mad at him; that he could never get things right. I had made him feel condemned because he misplaced his shoes. I can't even find my keys a lot of days and I condemned a four-year-old.

Then, Tom showed me what was in his little hand.

It was this drawing.

The little guy had drawn me a Father's Day picture to try to make me happy, to try to make me happy with him.

I was so wrong.

I picked Tom up and hugged him and told him, "No, Tom. Your daddy is wrong. I'm sorry. Will you forgive me?"

This lesson I learned the hard way—ask for forgiveness and forgive—goes hand-in-hand with Lesson #4, "You can't do it alone." Because people get on each other's nerves. We don't see eye to eye. We talk too much. We get things wrong. We do things that offend each other.

We must be quick to ask for forgiveness and quick to forgive.

Why?

Jesus instructed us in Mark 11:22-25 to:

> *Have faith in God. I tell you the truth, if anyone says to this mountain, "Go, throw yourself into the sea," and does not doubt in his heart but believes that what he says will happen, it will be done for him. Therefore I tell you, whatever you ask for in prayer, believe that you have received it, and it will be yours. And when you stand praying, if you hold anything against anyone, <u>forgive him, so that your Father in heaven may forgive you your sins.</u>*

Unforgiveness stops the Kingdom of God in your life. That alone should prevent forgiving others from ever being *optional* for you.

In Matthew 18:21-35, Jesus tells the parable of the unmerciful servant.

*Then Peter came to Jesus and asked, "Lord, how many times shall I forgive my brother when he sins against me? Up to seven times?"*

*Jesus answered, "I tell you, not seven times, but seventy-seven times.*

*Therefore, the kingdom of heaven is like a king who wanted to settle accounts with his servants. As he began the settlement, a man who owed him ten thousand talents was brought to him. Since he was not able to pay, the master ordered that he and his wife and his children and all that he had be sold to repay the debt.*

*The servant fell on his knees before him. 'Be patient with me,' he begged, 'and I will pay back everything.' The servant's master took pity on him, canceled the debt and let him go.*

*But when that servant went out, he found one of his fellow servants who owed him a hundred denarii. He grabbed him and began to choke him. 'Pay back what you owe me!' he demanded.*

*His fellow servant fell to his knees and begged him, 'Be patient with me, and I will pay you back.'*

*But he refused. Instead, he went off and had the man thrown into prison until he could pay the debt. When the other servants saw what had happened, they were greatly distressed and went and told their master everything that had happened.*

*Then the master called the servant in. 'You wicked servant,' he said, 'I canceled all that debt of yours because you begged me to. Shouldn't you have had mercy on your fellow servant just as I had on you?'*

*In anger his master turned him over to the jailers to be tortured, until he should pay back all he owed.*

*This is how my heavenly Father will treat each of you unless you forgive your brother from your heart."*

You and I are represented by the servant who had all of his debt forgiven. And, just like that guy, we have absolutely no excuse not to forgive others after all that we've been forgiven. If we don't forgive, we separate ourselves from God and give Satan an advantage over us (2 Corinthians 2:10-11).

And if stopping the Kingdom from advancing in your life, separating yourself from God, and giving the enemy an advantage over you aren't enough to make you go around forgiving everyone for everything, you should also know that unforgiveness is poison. It will eat at you from the inside out like a spiritual cancer. It will affect your health and every other relationship in your life, whether you intend it to or not.

It's life and death.

You must deal with it on both sides. Ephesians 4:26-27 say not to let the sun go down on your anger or give the devil any such foothold or opportunity. Say you're sorry to those you've hurt or offended, and forgive others quickly when you've been hurt or offended, whether they've said they were sorry or not.

Jesus told us to pray, *"Forgive us our debts, as we also have forgiven our debtors"* (Matthew 6:12). And He didn't mean financial debts.

Romans 13:8-10 say,

> *Let no debt remain outstanding, except the continuing debt to love one another, for he who loves his fellowman has fulfilled the law. The commandments, "Do not commit adultery," "Do not murder," "Do not steal," "Do not covet," and whatever other commandment there may be, are summed up in this one rule: "Love your neighbor as yourself." Love does no harm to its neighbor. Therefore love is the fulfillment of the law.*

We're expected to love others. There are multiple Scriptures that also tell us to feed our enemies, do good to those who hate us, bless those who curse us, and do good to those who mistreat us. Why? Because if you can feed someone and do good toward them, it demonstrates that you have no unforgiveness toward them.

See, Satan doesn't have to tempt you to murder someone or steal. He just has to get you offended and walking in unforgiveness. Then, he has you outside of love and outside of God's legal jurisdiction. That's why 1 Peter 3 says that husbands and wives need to walk in love with each other and not to let unforgiveness hinder their prayers.

We have the potential to pick up an offense every single day, multiple times a day—in traffic, with our family and friends, at our jobs, in line at the post office. In fact, offense is the most effective way the enemy pulls people out of the Kingdom, out of God's legal jurisdiction. And he's not going to stop trying. He'll keep using people to try to get you walking in unforgiveness, and he'll use you to offend others. No one is exempt. He even tried it with Jesus.

Don't give in.

Ask God to help you overlook offenses, and be quick to ask for forgiveness and to forgive.

# BE "THE WISE."
## YOU DON'T HAVE TO DO THINGS THE HARD WAY.

*Go back through Chapter Five and fill in the blanks from these important points.*

We must be quick to ask for _____ and quick to _____.

Jesus instructed us in Mark 11:22-25 to:

> *Have faith in God. I tell you the truth, if anyone says to this mountain, "Go, throw yourself into the sea," and does not doubt in his heart but believes that what he says will happen, it will be done for him. Therefore I tell you, whatever you ask for in prayer, believe that you have received it, and it will be yours. And when you stand praying, if you hold anything against anyone, _____ _____ _____.*

_____ stops the Kingdom of God in your life. That alone should prevent forgiving others from ever being _____ for you.

You and I are represented by the servant who had _____ of his debt forgiven.

If we don't forgive, we _____ ourselves from God and give Satan an _____ over us.

Unforgiveness is _____. It will eat you from the inside out like a spiritual cancer. It will affect your _____ and _____ other relationship in your life, whether you intend it to or not.

Jesus told us to pray, "*Forgive us our* _____, *as we also have* _____ *our debtors*" (Matthew 6:12). And He didn't mean _____ debts.

We're expected to _____ others.

If you can _____ someone and _____ _____ toward them, it demonstrates that you have no unforgiveness toward them.

Satan doesn't have to tempt you to murder or steal. He just has to get you _____ and walking in unforgiveness. Then, he has you outside of _____ and outside of God's _____ _____.

_____ is the most effective way the enemy pulls people out of the _____, out of God's legal jurisdiction.

## CONSIDER
### HAVE YOU BEEN DOING THIS THE HARD WAY?

In what areas of your life has God been telling you that you have a problem?

_____

_____

_____

_____

Describe a time you know you wrongly judged or condemned someone else:

_____

_____

_____

_____

Do you consider yourself quick to *ask for forgiveness*? Why, or why not?

_____

_____

_____

_____

Do you consider yourself quick to *forgive*? Why, or why not?

_____

_____

_____

_____

How do you feel when you read the parable of the unmerciful servant from Matthew 18:21-35?

_____

_____

_____

Write out 2 Corinthians 2:10-11:

How is unforgiveness poison to you and your relationships?

Write out Ephesians 4:26-27:

Summarize Romans 13:8-10 in your own words:

What does 1 Peter 3 say that husbands and wives need to do?

_____

_____

_____

_____

# CHALLENGE
## IT'S TIME TO TAKE ACTION.

Forgiveness. It's easy to say but not so easy to actually do. Many people will say they've forgiven because they've heard it's the right thing to do, and they *feel* like they've forgiven. But forgiveness isn't a feeling; it's a choice that requires corresponding action.

My wife, Drenda, walks people through this process:

Picture yourself standing face-to-face with the person who wounded you, rejected you, stole from you, or hurt you. Then, picture what you'd like to do to get even.

Yep. Go there for a minute. And if you're the person you're most angry with, picture yourself.

Now, just as you are ready to yell at the person, slap them, shoot them, reject them, cut them down with your words, or whatever it is you want to do...

Imagine Jesus stepping in front of you, standing between you and the person who has caused you so much pain. Looking into your eyes, He says compassionately to you, *"Whatever you want to do to them, do to Me instead. Unleash your hurt on Me. I paid for their sins, their offenses, and their mistakes, just as I paid for yours. What do you want to do to Me to get even with them for their offenses against you?"*

Ouch, right?

Because you're not going to inflict pain or nasty words on Jesus, are you?

So then He says, *"Forgive them as I have forgiven you. Turn them over to Me. Trust Me with this pain and hurt. Only I can be trusted to justify and judge. No man or woman has the righteous standing to make either decision. On the scales of justice, all men and women are guilty. My sacrifice is sufficient for you both."*

My friend, drop your weapons.

Release your pain and say, "Father, forgive them. I forgive them."

# PRAYER

Father, I thank You for Your gift of forgiveness. Help me tear down any walls of unforgiveness, bitterness, or jealousy that are keeping me from living the life You have planned for me. Help me never to let my emotions or memories control me, but to take every thought captive and make it obedient to Christ. I praise You for the work You are doing in my life, making me quick to ask for forgiveness and quick to forgive. In Jesus's name, amen.

Chapter Six

# YOU CAN BE FINANCIALLY FREE.

When Drenda and I were first married, we had no money. In fact, we had borrowed $500 from a friend to even get married, so we really started out in debt. We lived on commissions from my work with an insurance company, which I really believed in, but as you learned in Chapter Two, I was extremely shy and dreaded talking to people. So, you can imagine that that didn't go well with my insurance business.

But as you also learned from Chapter Two, courage isn't the *absence* of fear. No, courage is actually defined as the mental or moral strength to venture, persevere, and withstand danger, fear, or difficulty. *Courage is moving forward in the face of fear.*

So, I plodded through my fears, made my calls, and actually became pretty good at selling insurance. I was making decent money, and Drenda and I had some free time since I set my own appointments and most of those were in the evenings. It wasn't too long, however, before I found out that it takes money—*a lot of money*—to have things, do things, and to be able to function in life. My commissions were just not keeping up.

Not knowing better, we started using credit cards to buy what we needed. Then, when we ran out of credit card options, we used finance company loans to consolidate those cards. When money got tight again, we'd get new credit cards. We also had two car loans. Then, of course, we bought a house, which we didn't really qualify for. Drenda's parents loaned us the down payment, and my boss wrote a letter to the mortgage company, which actually exaggerated our income. The mortgage company approved the loan. But when the first payment came due, we didn't have it.

We scraped by. And when things broke, we used more debt.

Then, there were taxes. Working on commission means you pay your own taxes, and we didn't have the money to pay them, so I just didn't file. I really thought I'd get around to it when the money was there. But the money just never showed up. Eventually, we *had* to file, and we ended up owing *thousands* of dollars, which led to tax liens and extreme stress.

The bottom line is, after just six years of marriage, we had accumulated 10 maxed out and canceled credit credits, two car loans on old run-down and broken cars, three finance company loans at 23% interest, judgments filed against us, and thousands of dollars in tax liens. On top of that, we owed our parents tens of thousands of dollars, which we had borrowed just to survive.

Life was horribly stressful, and I was having trouble coping.

I ended up having panic attacks and being put on antidepressants. Not only that, but the stress caused me to deal with hypoglycemia as well, and doctors kept telling me I would end up being a diabetic.

One day, I woke up to find my body paralyzed. I couldn't move! Fear had a death grip on me. I lived so stressed out that I even became afraid to leave my house. My wife began to plan how she and our children would survive.

It was hell on earth. It wasn't living.

We had bought into the lies the media feeds us—to trust in debt and the earth curse system. Your parents may have even trained you to trust in debt, cosigning for your first car or helping you get your first credit card.

**Know this: Debt isn't designed to help you, and there's nothing unintentional about it. It's a well-thought-out plot to steal every ounce of your vision and your strength.**

I can remember one particular time I was expecting a paycheck in the mail for about $2,000 from a policy I had written. I needed that $2,000. That was big money to me back then, really big money.

Knowing the pay cycle of the insurance company and knowing that the insurance policy had been issued, I knew that the check would be in the mail in about five days. Banking on that, I wrote out about $2,000 worth of bills and mailed them off. I thought I had timed things perfectly.

But when Friday came, there was no check in the mail. I knew that most of those checks I had written would hit the bank that night. I was in trouble.

I didn't know what to do. Trying to come up with a quick plan, I had a brilliant idea: I would open a new checking account at a nearby bank and write a $2,000 check from the new, empty checking account. Then, I would deposit that check into the account the checks were going to hit that night. Do you see where this is going?

On Monday morning, I checked my account, and the plan had worked perfectly. All of the checks cleared that night as paid. Confident that the paycheck for $2,000 would be there, and I could get the whole situation remedied, I went to the post office.

But to my horror, the check wasn't there. So, now I had

another problem to solve.

Desperate, I figured the same strategy would work in reverse. So, this time, I wrote a check from my original bank account and deposited it into the new checking account I had only opened to perpetrate my plan. It worked again.

For some reason, that $2,000 paycheck didn't show up for *two* weeks. Two weeks. So, for two weeks, this was going on. And, in the meantime, other bills came in, and, of course, there were groceries to buy. So the $2,000 check quickly became about $2,600. And, each day, there I was going back and forth between the banks.

This continued until one morning when I received a call from one of the banks. I immediately recognized the voice on the phone. It was the branch manager I always talked to when I made my deposits. I had been sharing with her how knowing Jesus could change her life. I even had a Christian image printed on my checks.

There was no friendly open to this conversation.

"I know what you're doing!" she said. "I've closed your account, and you're to bring into the bank the full balance you owe us or we will press charges. And, by the way, you can never have an account at our bank again."

I can't even tell you how embarrassed and humiliated I was. Thankfully, the paycheck I had been waiting on finally showed up that day, and I was able to pay the bank all I owed. But I felt so much shame walking back into that bank and meeting with the branch manager. I told her I was sorry and that this was all *my* doing and that God had nothing to do with it; it was my own stupidity.

My life back then was full of these types of shameful events and financial despair. I *hated* being in debt, and I wondered what it might feel like to be free of debt. But I had little hope, so it was a real struggle to even imagine how that might feel.

As time went on, things only got worse. We had no groceries and often had to pawn the few things we had just to buy food. The IRS and bill collectors called us on a daily basis. We even ran out of heating oil for our house in the winter. There are so many stories I could share. I wish I could say that this was all just a bump in the road, or an anomaly, but it was our life for nine years!

I mentioned in the introduction to this book how I clearly remember the day I reached the end of my rope. An attorney had called us and said he had waited long enough for payment and was filing a lawsuit on behalf of his client. That call made me realize I was done; there were no more debt options left, no relatives that would give me one more penny. I had no options.

Feeling afraid and completely hopeless, I climbed the stairs to our little bedroom in the broken-down farmhouse, lay across the bed, and cried out to God. I was surprised when He answered very quickly. Up out of my spirit, I heard Him say, *"I had nothing to do with this mess. The reason you are in this mess is because you have not taken the time to learn how My Kingdom operates."*

There was more that He said to me that day, but I got the message: my mistake was trying to prosper the world's way, by using debt, and that wouldn't work.

God wanted to teach me how He pays for things—how His Kingdom operates. Of course, I had no clue what He was talking about at the time, but I was ready to learn.

I went downstairs and grabbed Drenda's hand and repented to her, and we both prayed and asked God to teach us how His Kingdom operated since we obviously didn't have a clue.

The attorney that had called that day said that in order to avoid the lawsuit, I would have to have $1,500 to him within three days. At the time, we had no money and no business in the pipeline that would pay out to us in time to take care of that. I didn't have a solution.

The next evening, I had an insurance sales call with a family, and I drove our old van to the appointment. I had been driving that old beat-up van for some time. There I was in financial sales, dressed in my suit, driving a rusted-out heap of a mess that would fill the whole road with white smoke as I pulled out from their houses.

I was so ashamed of that van that I would park it around the corner or a few blocks away, and then I'd walk to the clients' houses.

But this time, as I left, my client followed me out to the van. I got in the van, but I didn't want to start it and have it sputter and kick out smoke, so I just sat there with the window down, talking to him, and he stood there.

I knew I had to start the van. Sure enough, like usual, the whole road filled with white smoke. Well, that client just so happened to be a part-time mechanic. He quickly told me to turn the van off and he popped the hood. He poked around a bit and then came to my window and said, "You have a broken head gasket. Drive it home, and get it fixed as soon as possible."

Of course, I didn't need anyone to tell me the engine had a problem. That was obvious. What also was obvious was that I didn't have a dime to cover any repair.

On the way home, I prayed and talked to the Lord about this Kingdom thing and my van. Drenda and I had just made the commitment to really learn how the Kingdom of God operated, and I was stuck.

I said out loud, "Lord, I can't pay this van off. I can't fix it. I don't know. Maybe it would be better if it just burned up. I don't know, Lord!"

Of course, I didn't expect the thing to *really* burn up. I was just venting my frustration.

But seconds later, I noticed a little bubble on the hood that I didn't remember being there. And, as I drove, the bubble got bigger. Minutes later, the whole thing was on fire!

As I pulled into my office and brought the van to a stop, flames burst out of the engine compartment and rose six feet off of the hood. I was in shock as I ran into the building and called the fire department. It only took a few minutes for them to arrive, but it was too late.

To make a long story short, the van was totaled, and the insurance company gave me a settlement. After paying off the van loan, I was left with about $2,500—more than enough to overnight the attorney the $1,500. We even had money left to buy some groceries and pay a few other essential bills.

As we sat around the dinner table a few nights later, still shocked by what had happened, we realized we still needed a vehicle. My little, old sedan could only hold four people, and we were a family of six at the time.

Well, my dad heard the van story and called me. He told me to come to his house in the morning, and we would go looking for a vehicle. My hopes soared. My dad was wealthy and could easily write out a check for our new van.

The next morning, my dad and I went to a dealership and looked at all the options, and we found a van that we thought was perfect for my family. The price was about $19,000. My dad pulled me aside and told me that if I liked the van, he would give me $5,000 toward its purchase.

I didn't know what to do. My dad had no idea just how bad our financial situation was. But I knew I didn't have the credit to get a loan on the remaining balance for the van. So I had to tell my dad the truth. He quickly said that he would cosign for the van. I knew I didn't want to use debt after what the Lord told me, but I felt stuck. I went ahead and filled out a credit application, and the dealership said they would let us know if we had been approved by the next morning.

That night, Drenda and I couldn't sleep. We knew we couldn't go through with that purchase. But we also knew we needed a vehicle. By morning, we were sure we couldn't go through with using debt to buy the new van. We called the dealership and told them we wouldn't be picking up the van. Then, we called my dad and told him the same.

Now what? We didn't know.

During that time in our lives, Drenda would often stop at garage sales and look for things that we could buy and resell to make some cash. Her parents ran a monthly household auction in Georgia and would often make trips to Ohio to buy items and then resell them there. So Drenda was always looking for things to sell.

A few days after the van burned up, she received a call from a man that she had met months before. He had remembered her and somehow had kept her number. He worked at a nursing home and said that he had two rooms full of stuff that needed to be sold and cleared out and wondered if she was interested. Drenda said yes, called her parents about it, and they wired the money to buy the entire lot. Then, they came with a truck and took all of it back to Georgia and sold it at their auction. They did so well with the auction that they said they were going to give Drenda a commission on it.

The commission was a very clean, used station wagon. We were thrilled! We had a vehicle that was paid for, *for the first time in our lives*. We had eliminated the van debt and had learned a lesson in how God's Kingdom operated.

Remember how I said I hated being in debt, and I wondered what it might feel like to be free of debt, but I had little hope, so it was a real struggle to even imagine how that might feel?

Well, we found out financial freedom was a GREAT feeling.
God was training us that His ways were good and freeing. From that point on, we began to apply what God was teaching us to *every* area of our lives.

In just two and a half years, we became completely debt free. We began paying cash for new cars, building and paying for our dream home, and prospering at a level where we were actually giving hundreds of thousands of dollars to various ministry projects around the world.

Our lives drastically changed, but our memories of those nine dark years gave us a passion to teach people about the Kingdom of God. We *hate* poverty and lack.

Our story has a great ending, but the saddest part is that we NEVER had to go through those nine years of financial slavery and stress in the first place. We never had to learn the hard way how finances worked. We could've learned God's system from the very beginning and prospered.

That's our prayer for you—that you learn how life works God's way, without all the pain and stress.

God is the author of life, and He gave us the ultimate instruction manual: the Bible.

# BE "THE WISE."
## YOU DON'T HAVE TO DO THINGS THE HARD WAY.

*Go back through Chapter Six and fill in the blanks from these important points.*

The media feeds us lies—to trust in _____ and the_____ _____ system.

Debt isn't designed to _____ you, and there's nothing unintentional about it. It's a well-thought-out _____ to _____ every ounce of your _____ and _____.

God is the author of_____, and He gave us the ultimate_____ _____: the Bible.

How have you bought into the lies the media feeds us about trusting in debt?

<br>

<br>

<br>

Have you ever gotten caught up in a financial situation you didn't know how to get out of? What happened?

<br>

<br>

<br>

Describe a time when you feel you misrepresented God financially.

<br>

<br>

<br>

Do you believe you understand how God's Kingdom operates when it comes to faith and finances?

_____

_____

_____

_____

Are you trusting in the world's system of debt to maintain your current lifestyle?

_____

_____

_____

_____

Are you financially free? If so, how does it feel? If not, what do you imagine it might feel like to be free financially?

_____

_____

_____

_____

What do you know you need to do to learn more about God's system so you can prosper?

_____

_____

_____

## CHALLENGE
### IT'S TIME TO TAKE ACTION.

When Drenda and I started our company many years ago, we decided to give people a simple outline of the things they would need to do to get out of debt. With some time, effort, and thought, we eventually condensed our advice down to five basic, simple rules people need to master to change their financial future. They've worked for others, and they will work for you.

## Rule #1 - Seek First the Kingdom of God

Matthew 6:33 tells us that if we seek His Kingdom first, *"all these things will be given to you as well."* If we take the time to seek knowledge regarding His Kingdom and how it works, then we can access it and walk in it. For your life to change financially, you must take the time to study, write down, dissect, and understand the laws that govern the Kingdom of God, specifically in the area of finances.

## Rule #2 - Stop Using Debt

The debt system is one almost all of us were raised in, so naturally, it's the one we tend to trust in the most to meet our needs, especially when the going gets tough. But to walk in God's system, we must turn away from that old system.

- Set a budget.
- Live below your income level.
- Set goals for saving.
- Don't make impulsive purchases.

### Rule #3 – Cut Off Debt Options

You must get drastic with steps to protect yourself from ever being forced or tempted to use debt again. Acknowledge that you can't trust yourself in the early days of your decision to turn away from debt. Cancel the credit lines. Cut up the credit cards. Don't give yourself any room for error.

### Rule #4 – Give

Consistently through the New Testament, we see Jesus teaching about giving. Paul did so as well in 2 Corinthians 9:6-10. (Go study it.)

See, giving is the doorway that gives God the opening to bless you with opportunities, direction, concepts, and ideas that will propel your life financially. View the tithe as a fence. If you had a garden, and you had animals that would likely eat your produce, you would put up a fence. In a similar way, the tithe, as the Bible tells us, opens the windows of heaven and sets a guard around your financial life. But the fence doesn't grow anything itself. That's where offerings come in. Putting tithes and offerings into place allows God to bless the work of your hands.

### Rule #5 – Write Your Plan

Having a written plan that you can frequently refer back to, take direction from, and find comfort in will help you gain confidence that financial freedom is possible for you. A written plan will help you stay on track when life's pressures and temptations attempt to distract you.

Above all, remember that you *can* be financially free.

You can get more information about how to fix your money thing in my book, *Fixing the Money Thing: A Practical Guide to Financial Success.*

# PRAYER

Father, I praise You that You are the author of life, and that You gave us the ultimate instruction manual: the Bible. I ask for forgiveness for not taking the time to learn how Your Kingdom operates in regard to finances. I ask that You reveal to me any areas of my life where I've been trusting in the world's system of debt, the earth curse system. Help me to learn all about Your Kingdom system and to start operating in it from this moment on. Thank You for releasing Your promises into my life, and for complete financial freedom! In Jesus's name, amen.

# CONCLUSION

Life is all about learning. There are so many things we need to learn to prosper and live a fulfilling life.

These six chapters cover some of the things Drenda and I learned the hard way.

The hard way is the slow way, my friend. You don't have to learn that way.

It has been more than 27 years now since the van burned up, and Drenda and I are so thankful that we've walked in the blessings of the Kingdom ever since.

The Kingdom of God has taken us places that we never even dreamed of. It's hard to believe that the same two people that lived in that kind of dysfunction for so long now share the Good News of the Gospel and the message of financial freedom around the world and on television through our program, *Fixing the Money Thing*, that airs daily in every time zone on earth.

Know this: We are regular people, just like you; and if the Kingdom of God worked for us, it will work for *anyone*.

Remember, you don't have to do things the hard way. God's ways, His Kingdom laws, are available to anyone. You can discover real answers on how to release the Kingdom of God into YOUR life.

Visit faithlifenow.com for more information about the Kingdom of God, and for more strategies for success in the areas of faith, family, and finances.

# BE "THE WISE"
# ANSWER KEY

## Chapter One

Taking responsibility for someone when they need to take responsibility for themselves prevents them from feeling the "struggle" that will drive them to change and succeed.

Someone who has a heart to help can very quickly become an enabler, and the one who is supposedly being helped can become entitled.

If we're truly going to help people get better and win in life, we have to step back and help them identify where they need to grow, sow, and harvest for themselves.

Sometimes the very best thing is for a person to find himself or herself in a situation where they haven't taken the <u>time</u> or the <u>responsibility</u> they should have, and they're <u>hungry</u> (literally or figuratively.)

Proverbs 16:26 says, "*The laborer's appetite works <u>for</u> him; his <u>hunger</u> drives him on.*"

Drenda and I have learned to <u>ask questions</u> and to help the person in need with a <u>plan</u> that they are responsible for and then to hold them accountable to the plan before we just throw money at the problem.

You're not helping people by allowing them to continue in their <u>dysfunction</u>. You can be kind, gently instruct, love, and lead people to <u>take personal responsibility</u>.

When life isn't working, many times, if not most of the time, there are <u>spiritual </u>issues that must be dealt with as well.

## Chapter Two

The devil operates by presenting false <u>evidence</u>—shadows, smokescreens, and setups—to scare you. He doesn't want you to know who you are, and he wants to steal every bit of <u>courage</u> from you that he can. Because he knows that as long as you're operating in <u>fear</u>, you'll stay zipped up in your tent, unable to discern the truth.

The enemy isn't looking to devour unbelievers. He already has them. No, he's looking to devour believers. He's looking to devour <u>you</u>, one bite—one <u>lie</u>, one <u>deception</u>—at a time.

But the enemy has already been defeated. So, as a believer, the real battle occurs in your <u>mind</u>.

Courage isn't the <u>absence</u> of fear. No, courage is actually defined as the mental or moral strength to venture, persevere, and withstand danger, fear, or difficulty. Courage is <u>moving</u> <u>forward</u> in the face of fear.

Just like Joshua, you have to have <u>courage</u> to go into new territory, and to lead people to someplace they've never been. <u>Faith</u> can take you to the edge, but it's <u>courage</u> that helps you take the leap.

Courage is a <u>choice</u>, a decision to move forward in the face of fear.

You can be courageous not because of who you are, but because of who <u>God</u> is.

It's courage combined with <u>faith</u> for your God-inspired <u>vision</u> that releases the <u>anointing</u> of God.

The enemy isn't interested in a fraction. He doesn't just want an inch or a mile; he wants your <u>entire</u> <u>life</u>.

## Chapter Three

God never said things would be <u>easy</u>; He just said all things are possible.

God has a system in place to <u>change</u> us, <u>mature</u> us, and <u>train</u> us, and most of it won't be comfortable or easy or instant.

Most of us launch out into things in <u>faith</u>, having heard from God, but then we somehow end up in places where we're trying to do it in our own <u>strength.</u>

If you're going to do anything God wants you to do in your life, you will absolutely face <u>pressure</u> and uncomfortable, tough <u>decisions</u>.

Start now knowing that there are going to be things that don't look possible, because they're not <u>without</u> <u>God</u>.

There will be <u>pressure</u> when you launch out on a God-idea, but pressure isn't your enemy. Pressure usually leads to <u>frustration</u>, and frustration is the breeding ground of <u>change</u>.

When you push forward through the pressure, you'll find your <u>victory</u>, and your <u>future</u>, on the other side.

In God's Kingdom, it just gets <u>bigger</u>.

For most of us, the processes we currently operate by limit our capacity for increase.

In order to increase anything in your life, you have to allow the Holy Spirit to help you change or correct your processes, how you do things.

We all need to be stretched.

God doesn't get maxed out, and He looks at you from the same perspective. God brings more opportunities when we say yes.

The pressure of those opportunities can easily make us say no, but then we'll quit advancing.

The harvest will always be too big for you and your capacity. You have to work with God, and you have to let Him stretch you.


## Chapter Four

Running away, backing up, hiding out, or trying to escape weren't options. They're never the answer. Engaging is.

Love requires action.

If you really love Jesus, you're going to do what He says. If you really love your spouse, you're going to be concerned about his or her world and <u>show</u> it.

God doesn't want you to do life alone. He created you for <u>relationship</u>, with Him and with others.

You need <u>people</u>, and people need <u>you</u>.


## **Chapter Five**

We must be quick to ask for <u>forgiveness</u> and quick to <u>forgive</u>.

Jesus instructed us in Mark 11:22-25 to:

> *Have faith in God. I tell you the truth, if anyone says to this mountain, "Go, throw yourself into the sea," and does not doubt in his heart but believes that what he says will happen, it will be done for him. Therefore I tell you, whatever you ask for in prayer, believe that you have received it, and it will be yours. And when you stand praying, if you hold anything against anyone, <u>forgive him, so that your Father in heaven may forgive you your sins.</u>*

<u>Unforgiveness</u> stops the Kingdom of God in your life. That alone should prevent forgiving others from ever being <u>optional</u> for you.

You and I are represented by the servant who had <u>all</u> of his debt forgiven.

If we don't forgive, we <u>separate</u> ourselves from God and give Satan an <u>advantage</u> over us.

Unforgiveness is <u>poison</u>. It will eat you from the inside out like a spiritual cancer. It will affect your <u>health</u> and <u>every</u> other relationship in your life, whether you intend it to or not.

Jesus told us to pray, "*Forgive us our <u>debts</u>, as we also have <u>forgiven</u> our debtors*" (Matthew 6:12). And He didn't mean <u>financial</u> debts.

We're expected to <u>love</u> others.

If you can <u>feed</u> someone and <u>do</u> <u>good</u> toward them, it demonstrates that you have no unforgiveness toward them.

Satan doesn't have to tempt you to murder or steal. He just has to get you <u>offended</u> and walking in unforgiveness. Then, he has you outside of <u>love</u> and outside of God's <u>legal</u> <u>jurisdiction</u>.

<u>Offense</u> is the most effective way the enemy pulls people out of the <u>Kingdom</u>, out of God's legal jurisdiction.

## Chapter Six

The media feeds us lies—to trust in <u>debt</u> and the <u>earth</u> <u>curse</u> system.

Debt isn't designed to <u>help</u> you, and there's nothing unintentional about it; it's a well-thought-out <u>plot</u> to <u>steal</u> every ounce of your <u>vision</u> and <u>strength</u>.

God is the author of <u>life</u>, and He gave us the ultimate <u>instruction</u> <u>manual</u>: the Bible.